SOME MAJOR EVENTS IN WORLD WAR II

THE EUROPEAN THEATER

1939 SEPTEMBER—Germany invades Poland Great Britain, France, Australia, & New Zealand declare war on Germany; Battle of the Atlantic begins. NOVEMBER—Russia invades Finland.

1940 APRIL—Germany invades Denmark & Norway. MAY—Germany invades Belgium, Luxembourg, & The Netherlands; British forces retreat to Dunkirk and escape to England. JUNE—Italy declares war on Britain & France; France surrenders to Germany. JULY—Battle of Britain begins. SEPTEMBER—Italy invades Egypt; Germany, Italy, & Japan form the Axis countries. OCTOBER—Italy invades Greece. NOVEMBER—Battle of Britain over. DECEMBER—Britain attacks Italy in North Africa.

1941 JANUARY—Allies take Tobruk. FEBRUARY—Rommel arrives at Tripoli. APRIL—Germany invades Greece & Yugoslavia. JUNE—Allies are in Syria; Germany invades Russia. JULY—Russia joins Allies. AUGUST—Germans capture Kiev. OCTOBER—Germany reaches Moscow. DECEMBER—Germans retreat from Moscow; Japan attacks Pearl Harbor; United States enters war against Axis nations.

1942 MAY—first British bomber attack on Cologne. JUNE—Germans take Tobruk. SEPTEMBER—Battle of Stalingrad begins. OCTOBER—Battle of El Alamein begins. NOVEMBER—Allies recapture Tobruk; Russians counterattack at Stalingrad.

1943 JANUARY—Allies take Tripoli. FEBRUARY—German troops at Stalingrad surrender. APRIL—revolt of Warsaw Ghetto Jews begins. MAY—German and Italian resistance in North Africa is over; their troops surrender in Tunisia; Warsaw Ghetto revolt is put down by Germany. JULY—allies invade Sicily; Mussolini put in prison. SEPTEMBER—Allies land in Italy; Italians surrender; Germans occupy Rome; Mussolini rescued by Germany. OCTOBER—Allies capture Naples; Italy declares war on Germany. NOVEMBER—Russians recapture Kiev.

1944 JANUARY—Allies land at Anzio. JUNE—Rome falls to Allies; Allies land in Normandy (D-Day). JULY—assassination attempt on Hitler fails. AUGUST—Allies land in southern France. SEPTEMBER—Brussels freed. OCTOBER—Athens liberated. DECEMBER—Battle of the Bulge.

1945 JANUARY—Russians free Warsaw. FEBRUARY—Dresden bombed. APRIL—Americans take Belsen and Buchenwald concentration camps; Russians free Vienna; Russians take over Berlin; Mussolini killed; Hitler commits suicide. MAY—Germany surrenders; Goering captured.

THE PACIFIC THEATER

1940 SEPTEMBER—Japan joins Axis nations Germany & Italy.

1941 APRIL—Russia & Japan sign neutrality pact. DECEMBER—Japanese launch attacks against Pearl Harbor, Hong Kong, the Philippines, & Malaya; United States and Allied nations declare war on Japan; China declares war on Japan, Germany, & Italy; Japan takes over Guam, Wake Island, & Hong Kong; Japan attacks Burma.

1942 JANUARY—Japan takes over Manila; Japan invades Dutch East Indies. FEBRUARY—Japan takes over Singapore; Battle of the Java Sea. APRIL—Japanese overrun Bataan. MAY—Japan takes Mandalay; Allied forces in Philippines surrender to Japan; Japan takes Corregidor; Battle of the Coral Sea. JUNE—Battle of Midway; Japan occupies Aleutian Islands. AUGUST—United States invades Guadalcanal in the Solomon Islands.

1943 FEBRUARY—Guadalcanal taken by U.S. Marines. MARCH—Japanese begin to retreat in China. APRIL—Yamamoto shot down by U.S. Air Force. MAY—U.S. troops take Aleutian Islands back from Japan. JUNE—Allied troops land in New Guinea. NOVEMBER—U.S. Marines invade Bougainville & Tarawa.

1944 FEBRUARY—Truk liberated. JUNE—Saipan attacked by United States. JULY—battle for Guam begins. OCTOBER—U.S. troops invade Philippines; Battle of Leyte Gulf won by Allies.

1945 JANUARY—Luzon taken; Burma Road won back. MARCH—Iwo Jima freed. APRIL—Okinawa attacked by U.S. troops; President Franklin Roosevelt dies; Harry S. Truman becomes president. JUNE—United States takes Okinawa. AUGUST—atomic bomb dropped on Hiroshima; Russia declares war on Japan; atomic bomb dropped on Nagasaki. SEPTEMBER—Japan surrenders.

WORLD AT WAR

Resistance
Movements

WORLD AT WAR

Resistance
Movements

By R. Conrad Stein

Consultant:
    Professor Robert L. Messer, Ph.D.
    Department of History
    University of Illinois at Chicago Circle

 CHILDRENS PRESS, CHICAGO

In August, 1940, two months after France fell to the Germans, Adolf Hitler stood next to a long-range gun on the French channel coast. The gun was pointed toward England.

FRONTISPIECE: Danish resistors cover an attempted escape from a German-controlled Copenhagen jail in 1944.

Library of Congress Cataloging in Publication Data

Stein, R. Conrad.
  Resistance movements.

  (World at war)
  Includes index.
  Summary: Discusses the importance of resistance movements which sprang up in Yugoslavia, France, Russia, Greece, and other countries under German occupation during World War II.
  1. World War, 1939–1945—Underground movements —Juvenile literature. [1. World War, 1939–1945—Underground movements] I. Title. II. Series.
D802.A2S73 1982   940.53   82-9399
ISBN 0-516-04798-1   AACR2

PICTURE CREDITS:
UPI: Cover, pages 6, 9, 11, 12, 13, 14, 16, 17, 18, 19, 20, 22, 25, 28, 29, 30, 32, 33, 34, 39 (bottom right), 40, 42, 46 (top)
WIDE WORLD PHOTOS: Pages 4, 10, 23, 26, 35, 36, 39 (top and bottom left), 41, 45, 46 (bottom)

COVER PHOTO: Members of the French Forces of the Interior snipe from a window as French men and women tried to retake Paris from the Germans during the week before Allied troops liberated the city on August 25, 1944.

PROJECT EDITOR:
Joan Downing

CREATIVE DIRECTOR:
Margrit Fiddle

In the winter of 1941, German dictator Adolf Hitler enjoyed great military success. His armies occupied France and Belgium. To the east, the German war machine had taken Poland, Yugoslavia, and Greece. And German soldiers had swept over the plains of Russia to bang on the gates of Moscow.

At the height of his power, Hitler ruled over millions of people and thousands of square miles of territory. His forces had destroyed hundreds of armies in the field. But they had not shaken the will of the people whose countries they occupied. As long as foreign soldiers camped on their soil, the people fought back.

Across Europe, resistance movements sprang up. These groups of people resisted, or fought, the soldiers occupying their countries. The resistance movements did much to weaken Germany. Small bands of resistors fighting in the rear areas often did more damange than a division at the front.

At first, the conquered peoples of Europe fought back with "passive" resistance. They refused to obey orders. They ignored the enemy soldiers.

In 1940, the Germans ordered the French to take all Allied airmen to German headquarters. But the French people disobeyed those orders. They hid the Allied airmen who had parachuted out of damaged planes. Brave French men and women led the airmen to the English Channel and put them on boats going to England. Those airmen were able to fly more missions against Germany. The men and women protecting the airmen did so at the risk of their own lives. Any who were caught by the Germans would be shot.

In Denmark, the people also used passive resistance to frustrate their conquerors. Germany invaded Denmark in 1940. During their occupation, the Germans ordered all Jews to wear a band on one arm. The band was to have a Jewish religious symbol, the Star of David, on it. The day after the Germans issued the order,

German shock troops marched through a town in Denmark (left) as the Nazis invaded that country in April, 1940. King Christian X (right), along with most of the rest of his countrymen, found many ways to frustrate the Germans during their occupation.

seventy-year-old King Christian X of Denmark left his palace wearing a Star of David on his arm. Soon, practically every man, woman, and child in Copenhagen defiantly wore a Star of David. The Germans could not arrest them all, and the order was dropped. Later, brave Danish people hid Jews in their homes to protect them from the Nazis.

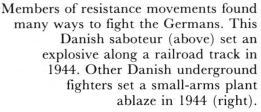
Members of resistance movements found many ways to fight the Germans. This Danish saboteur (above) set an explosive along a railroad track in 1944. Other Danish underground fighters set a small-arms plant ablaze in 1944 (right).

As the war dragged on, resistors stopped using passive resistance and began using active resistance. At times, more battles raged behind German lines than on the front.

Resistance movements attracted strong leaders. A few of those leaders brought their countries through the war and later became presidents and prime ministers.

A powerful resistance movement rose in Yugoslavia. The Germans marched into Yugoslavia in 1941. In the very first days of German occupation, Yugoslavian citizens struck back. Groups of people, often armed only with clubs, ambushed German soldiers. In the countryside, Yugoslavians blew up bridges and railroad tracks. The Germans reacted savagely. They issued an order stating that for every German killed they would round up and shoot fifty Yugoslavian civilians.

Armed German soldiers searched these Yugoslav patriots for weapons in the spring of 1943. The guerrillas were caught in the mountains, where they were operating against the Nazis.

Though the Germans encouraged the Serbs and Croats in Yugoslavia to fight each other, they did favor the Croatian fascists. These German troops were capturing "a band of Communists" who they claimed were terrorizing Croatian mountain dwellers.

The Germans also tried to divide the people of Yugoslavia. For many years Yugoslavia had been a country of several different national groups. Each group wanted its own homeland. The two largest national groups were the Croats and the Serbs. The Germans encouraged the Croats and Serbs to fight one another. They appointed an anti-Serbian fanatic named Ante Pavelich to rule over a newly created state of Croatia. Pavelich was a Croatian fascist who hated Serbs, Jews, and gypsies. He was such a cold-hearted killer that he shocked even the German officers. In 1941 a civil war broke out between the Croats and the Serbs. The Germans did little to stop the war. They believed that

Partisan Marshal Tito (left) with Colonel General
Kocha Popovitch, chief of the Yugoslav general staff.

while the Yugoslavians were busy shooting each
other they would be unable to shoot Germans.

A Yugoslavian leader named Drazha
Mihailovich rose up and organized a band of
resistors called the Chetniks. They fought the
Germans, but the Yugoslavian people continued
fighting each other.

It took an iron-willed leader to unite the
Yugoslavian people and turn their attention back
to fighting the Germans. In the confusion of the
civil war, such a leader emerged. His name was
Josip Broz. History remembers him as Marshal
Tito.

Tito was born a Croatian peasant. As a young
man he became a Communist. Soon after

This patrol of Tito's Yugoslav Partisans was on its way to fight Nazi occupation forces somewhere in Yugoslavia.

German occupation, Tito organized a resistance band he called the Partisans. The Partisans were highly mobile troops who often operated behind enemy lines.

At first, the Partisans had only a few rifles and very little food. But Tito's soldiers quickly learned to take supplies from their enemies.

Opposing the Partisans were the Germans and the Yugoslavian National Guard. Members of the national guard had little heart for the fight. In fact, the guardsmen were sometimes called "Partisan supply units." As Tito explained, "we catch them and take all their clothes and weapons, then send them home naked to be reequipped and captured again." The Partisans also took supplies from the Germans. On raids, the Partisans stole German rifles and ammunition. By the end of 1942, they had even managed to capture four tanks and three light bombers.

Hitler sent orders that one hundred Yugoslavians were to be killed for every German killed by a Partisan. The Yugoslavian war became a dreadful bloodbath. Both sides executed their prisoners, and the number of people shot was appalling. A Partisan raid on the town of Kraljevo killed 30 Germans. German forces retaliated by putting 1,700 civilians to death. The Partisans next killed 10 Germans at the town of Kragujevac. Because of that raid, 2,300 townsmen were executed. Most of the people killed had nothing to do with Partisan activity. They were simply dragged out of their homes, lined up against the wall, and shot.

One of every five of Tito's Partisans was a woman.

Through this bitter fighting, the Partisans and Tito grew steadily stronger. Often the brutal German tactics produced new recruits for Tito. Men and women whose families had been executed joined the Partisans to seek revenge.

One of every five of Tito's Partisans was a woman. The women fought side by side with the men. Some 25,000 women Partisans were killed during the course of the war.

Hitler called Tito a "bandit." The Germans offered a reward of $40,000 in gold for his capture. It is no wonder the Germans wanted

British Prime Minister Winston Churchill (left) sent his son Randolph to talk to Tito at his cave headquarters in the mountains (right).

Tito. By 1943, Germany had pulled fourteen divisions—about 140,000 men—away from other fronts and sent them to Yugoslavia to fight the Partisans.

At first, Western powers distrusted Tito because he was a Communist. But throughout the war years, British Prime Minister Winston Churchill often said, "Whoever marches with Hitler is a foe; whoever marches against him is a friend." Churchill ordered his own son Randolph to parachute into Tito's mountain headquarters and talk to him. Randolph Churchill brought

The British Royal Air Force officer at the right in the picture operated with Tito's Partisan forces in Yugoslavia.

back an impressive report on Tito. The British began shipping supplies to the Partisans through secret bases in the Mediterranean.

By the war's end, the Yugoslavian Partisans were no longer a small hit-and-run unit. Thousands of well-armed men and women served under Tito. Tito liberated large areas of Yugoslavia from German rule. After the war, Tito became president of Yugoslavia. For thirty-five years he was a one-man ruler of his country. Tito died on May 4, 1980.

After the fall of France, German soldiers paraded down the Champs Elysees in Paris on August 10, 1940.

A famous liberation movement also rose in France.

In 1940, France fell to the mighty German army. German soldiers paraded down the boulevard in Paris called the Champs Elysees. Many French onlookers watched in tears as the triumphant Germans marched down the streets of Paris.

Charles de Gaulle (left) is shown in London in July, 1940, as he was forming the Free French resistance movement.

But the French soon began fighting back. The motto of the French resistance was: "France has lost a battle; she has not lost the war."

Just days after the Germans entered Paris, a little-known French army officer made a radio address from London. The officer had recently escaped to England. He said, "Whatever happens, the flame of French resistance must not be quenched and will not be quenched." That officer's name was Charles de Gaulle. He became the most famous man in modern French history.

In England, de Gaulle formed an organization called the Free French. It became the command post of the French resistance. From London, de Gaulle made radio broadcasts to his home country. The Germans forbade the French to listen to these broadcasts, but the people listened anyway.

Under the encouragement of de Gaulle, the French resistance operated in the cities and the countryside. Spying on the Germans was one of its most important tasks. Using secret radios, resistors reported all German troop movements to England. Soon the Germans were unable to move even a company of troops without the French knowing about it. The Free French also sabotaged trains and supply dumps.

New recruits joined the resistance when the Germans began rounding up young men, shipping them to Germany, and forcing them to work in factories and mines. In order to escape this slave labor, many Frenchmen joined the resistance.

Above: Members of the French resistance learned how to assemble a machine gun blindfolded. Below right: Just before the fall of France, members of the underground blew up a French railway bridge in an attempt to stall the German advance. Below left: Michele Pernet (shown after the war), who earned the name "the Terrorist" while she worked for the French underground, was captured and tortured by the Germans.

The French patriots who derailed and set afire this German gasoline supply train (above) tied up the railroad line for five days. Another group of French resistors blew up the German barracks in Grenoble (below) when the Germans refused to release hostages.

Different elements of French society cooperated with the Free French. The resistance group published many secret newspapers. These were often distributed by French schoolchildren. Spies and saboteurs needed documents to be able to travel in occupied France. City police departments forged those documents for the Free French.

In the United States, the French resistance became very popular. Books and movies were written about the heroic resistors. The books and movies portrayed the work of the resistance as being glorious. But the Free French were really soldiers. A soldier in war does not find glory. He finds fear, suffering, and death.

In many ways the life of a resistor was worse than that of a combat soldier. A soldier, now and then, is pulled out of battle. At least for a few days he is not under fire. The resistor's life, on the other hand, was one of constant terror. A resistor could be arrested while crossing the

During their occupation of France, German troops rounded up hundreds of French citizens every day, both to instill fear and to hunt for underground members.

street, or he could be shaken out of bed at midnight. Fear followed the resistor like a shadow.

The German secret police, called the Gestapo, tried to stop the Free French. The Gestapo captured men and women of the resistance and tortured them to get information about other members of the Free French. The tortures were so awful that many people told the Gestapo what they wanted to know. Others remained silent until death.

After D-Day, members of the French resistance fought in the open after years of underground combat. The men above left their homes to join one of the fighting groups. The men below helped British and Canadian troops wipe out German snipers in the town of Quillebeuf.

On the eve of the great Allied invasion of Europe on June 6, 1944, Free French radio sent code messages to the French resistance. The Germans could hear the messages, but could make no sense of them. The messages were nothing more than random sentences thrown together: "John loves Mary. . . . Napoleon's hat is in the ring. . . . The arrow will not pass. . . ." But these sentences in gibberish made sense to the few French resistors who knew the secret code.

On the evening of June 5, 1944, the resistance leaders heard the news they had been awaiting for four years: "It is hot in Suez" and "The dice are on the table." Those two sentences meant the Allies were about to launch D-Day. The French resistance sprang into action.

During D-Day, the French resistance was a nightmare to the Germans. Operating behind the invasion beaches, they cut telephone lines, destroyed railroad tracks, and blew up bridges. German generals were unable to communicate with their field units. They were also unable to

General Dwight Eisenhower, supreme commander of the Allied Expeditionary Force, showed delight at the news of the liberation of Paris on August 25, 1944.

bring reinforcements to the beaches. The Allies rolled away from the beaches and swept across France. General Dwight Eisenhower later said that the French resistance had been worth fifteen army divisions to the Allied success.

On August 25, 1944, Allied forces liberated Paris. Once more, triumphant soldiers marched down the tree-lined boulevard called the Champs Elysees. But this time they were Free French soldiers. One of their leaders was Charles de Gaulle. After the war he became president of France.

Above: Members of the French resistance kept watch for German snipers in the streets of Paris three weeks before Allied troops entered the city.
Below: Three days after Paris was freed, a crowd gathered as General de Gaulle attended a reception in the Place de l'Hotel de Ville. During the reception scattered German snipers shot at the civilians and Allied troops gathered there.

Shortly after the German invasion of Russia, German troops captured this
group of Red Army men, who sit huddled near the field gun they were manning.

In occupied Russia, a resistance force of half a million men and women developed behind German lines.

Germany attacked Russia in 1941. At first the Germans enjoyed dizzying success. In a few months they occupied thousands of square miles of Russian territory. Early in the war, Russian civilians tolerated the Germans. In the central Russian area called the Ukraine, the people actually welcomed the German soldiers. The Ukrainians were staunchly anti-Communist. For years they had hoped to break away from Russia and establish their own homeland. But to the German command the Ukrainians were *untermenschen*—inferior people. The Ukrainians and Germans quickly became enemies, and the Ukrainians joined the Russians to form a fierce, fighting partisan (underground) army.

Early partisan fighters in Russia were Russian army troops who had been trapped behind their own lines. The initial German advance was so swift that the Germans encircled more Russians

German troops fighting in Russia faced the most terrible winters they had ever known. By the winter of 1943, the Russian partisans had made things even worse by cutting off the German lines of supply. Hitler's soldiers soon ran out of warm clothing, food, and ammunition.

than they could capture. The Russian soldiers, cut off from their own men, formed a new front behind the German lines. Later those soldiers were joined by Soviet civilians who wanted to drive the Germans out of their country.

Because Russia is such a vast country, the Germans had tremendously long supply lines. Supplies had to be shipped more than a thousand miles over the Russian countryside. Most of the German supplies were shipped by train. In 1943, Russian partisans declared war on the railroads. By the end of that year, the partisans claimed these achievements: 1,014 trains wrecked or derailed, 814 locomotives destroyed, 72 railroad bridges blown up.

These Soviet partisans, deep within Nazi-occupied Russia, stopped near a farmhouse to get something to eat and find out the strength of the German troops in the area.

Again the Germans reacted savagely to the partisan attacks. They knew the partisans were being supported largely by the farmers and village people. So the Germans took their revenge on those civilians. Civilians who are unlucky enough to be in the middle of a battleground usually suffer more than soldiers. An order from a German general called for fifty to one hundred Russian death sentences for the death of one German soldier.

In 1944 the Russian army launched a powerful offensive. The German forces reeled backwards. By that time, Russian resistance had grown very strong. Units of partisans were capturing towns two or three days ahead of their advancing army. The actions of the partisans helped the Russian army drive the Germans out of their country.

The Russian woman partisan shown below helped in the killing of 160 German troops during a raid on this village.

The German sign on a wall in Greece during the early days of occupation says "We will force you to your knees."

Greece also became a battleground where partisans and Axis armies fought.

Germany conquered Greece in 1941. The feared German flag, the swastika, flew over the city of Athens. The swastika was a symbol of rule by force. It was both ironic and tragic that the swastika should fly over Athens, the city where democracy was born.

These Italian troops, who occupied much of the countryside in Greece, were trying to move equipment and supplies to the front lines through hub-deep mud.

Even though the Germans held Athens, much of the Greek countryside was occupied by Italian troops. The Italians at the time were allied with the Germans. At first, resistance movements in Greece fought against Italian soldiers.

One Greek resistance movement was led by a man named Napoleon Zervas. Zervas did not look like a partisan leader. He liked to go to parties and eat rich Greek pastries. And he was overweight. Still, he had a sharp mind and commanded the loyalty of his troops.

In an early operation, Zervas and about a hundred of his followers prepared to ambush an Italian supply column. Zervas ordered his men to dig in on both sides of a canyon wall. His men looked down on an important mountain road. Buried in the road were powerful mines. The Italian supply column drove directly into Zervas's trap. With a thunderous roar, a mine blew up the lead tank. Zervas's men fired their rifles at the trucks. In a short time, the supply column had been totally destroyed.

The British were anxious to help the Greek resistors. In 1942, the British were fighting German forces in North Africa. The Germans supplied their North African army through ports in occupied Greece. The British hoped to be able to slow down the movement of German supplies to Africa.

In the fall of 1942, a team of eight British soldiers parachuted into the mountains of central Greece. They were led by a colonel named Eddie Meyers. His orders were to join the Greek partisans and blow up a huge railroad bridge that spanned a gorge in the mountains. It took more than a month for the British soldiers and the Greek partisans to work out their plan. But when they finally launched their attack, they were able to demolish the bridge with explosives within an hour and a half.

After the bridge was destroyed, Colonel Meyers remained in Greece. He became famous for his assistance to the partisans.

The Greek partisans stepped up their attacks, and the Germans had to pull troops away from other fronts to fight in Greece. The Germans quickly learned that they were up against a tough foe. Many of the Greek resistors were shepherds who knew every inch of their mountainous home. A frustrated German officer wrote, "Each footpath in the mountains, each path in the underbrush is familiar to them. . . . During the entire period of occupation hardly a night. . . and not a single day passed without a surprise attack, a mine explosion, or another act of sabotage occurring."

Top and left: Armed guerrillas
on the Greek island of Crete.
Above: This Greek woman fought
with a band of patriots for a
year before the Nazis were
driven from her homeland.

Bearded partisan leader Aris Velouchiotis with his fifteen-year-old aide, Louis Petropoulagos. Petropoulagos had gone through fifteen battles against the Nazis when this picture was taken in 1944.

But the ancient Greek tendency to fight among themselves weakened the partisans. The two most powerful partisan leaders—Zervas and Aris Velouchiotis—each dreamed of taking power in Greece when the war was over. Velouchiotis was a Communist. Zervas was an anti-Communist. Soon a confusing three-way war erupted. The forces of Zervas and Velouchiotis fought with each other. Both sides fought against the Germans.

These Greek partisans were on their way to join Allied units in their campaign to drive the Germans out of Greece.

In 1944, German troops had to retreat from Greece or be trapped by the oncoming Russian army. The Greeks continued fighting among themselves. Winston Churchill sent 50,000 British troops to try to stop the Greek civil war. Churchill was afraid of a Communist takeover in Greece. It was an ugly chapter in the story of Greek resistance.

Above: An armed partisan and civilians looked on as a British parachutist pinned the Union Jack on the arm of a small Greek boy.
Below: Greek guerrilla fighters lined up on the dock at Athens to welcome disembarking Canadian forces.

But Greek partisans had severely crippled the German war effort. The dreaded swastika no longer flew over the city of Athens where democracy had flourished more than two thousand years earlier.

Members of resistance movements fought in every occupied country during World War II. The Home Army in Poland battled the German occupiers. Resistors in Norway sabotaged a heavy water factory, thereby delaying a German atomic bomb project. In Italy, resistors captured and executed Mussolini. A resistance movement in Czechoslovakia led to a brutal German retaliation in which more than ten thousand Czechs were murdered.

In the Far East, resistance movements also rose up. Philippine freedom fighters waged almost constant warfare against the Japanese. In China, the Communist leader Mao Tse-Tung drove the Japanese army out of large sections of his country.

And many acts of resistance were performed by people who were not part of any movement. Even in Germany, brave German men and women risked their lives to help Jews escape from the Nazis. History will never know the names of most of those fearless Germans. Many were killed by the Nazis, and others had to live secret lives.

By the spring of 1945, the once-mighty German Empire had collapsed. No longer could Hitler look at a map of Europe and see huge territories the German Army had conquered. Instead, German soldiers were frantically defending the borders of their homeland. Hitler, hidden in a bunker in Berlin, committed suicide. In May, 1945, the long and terrible war in Europe came to an end. By September, the war in the Pacific was over.

All over the world, partisans put down their weapons and returned to peaceful work. Their struggle had helped free their countries and end World War II.

Only a few days after Adolf Hitler and Eva Braun had committed suicide, this American private inspected the site outside the bunker where their bodies had been burned.

Above: Only one week after Germany surrendered on May 7, 1945, these cheering Danes greeted British airborne fighters who had just come from the fighting in Germany. Below: In September of 1944, these members of the Dutch underground (P.A.N.) posed on a captured German People's car in the Eindhoven area.

Index

About the Author

Mr. Stein was born and grew up in Chicago. At eighteen he enlisted in the Marine Corps where he served three years. He was a sergeant at discharge. He later received a B.A. in history from the University of Illinois and an M.F.A. from the University of Guanajuato in Mexico.

Although he served in the Marines, Mr. Stein believes that wars are a dreadful waste of human life. He agrees with a statement once uttered by Benjamin Franklin: "There never was a good war or a bad peace." But wars are all too much a part of human history. Mr. Stein hopes that some day there will be no more wars to write about.